THE WORLD OF OCEAN ANIMALS
GREAT WHITE SHARKS

by Mari Schuh

Ideas for Parents and Teachers

Pogo Books let children practice reading informational text while introducing them to nonfiction features such as headings, labels, sidebars, maps, and diagrams, as well as a table of contents, glossary, and index.

Carefully leveled text with a strong photo match offers early fluent readers the support they need to succeed.

Before Reading

- "Walk" through the book and point out the various nonfiction features. Ask the student what purpose each feature serves.
- Look at the glossary together. Read and discuss the words.

Read the Book

- Have the child read the book independently.
- Invite him or her to list questions that arise from reading.

After Reading

- Discuss the child's questions. Talk about how he or she might find answers to those questions.
- Prompt the child to think more. Ask: Great white sharks have strong senses. How do their senses help them hunt?

Pogo Books are published by Jump!
5357 Penn Avenue South
Minneapolis, MN 55419
www.jumplibrary.com

Copyright © 2024 Jump!
International copyright reserved in all countries. No part of this book may be reproduced in any form without written permission from the publisher.

Library of Congress Cataloging-in-Publication Data

Names: Schuh, Mari C., 1975- author.
Title: Great white sharks / by Mari Schuh.
Description: Minneapolis, MN: Jump!, Inc., [2024]
Series: The world of ocean animals | Includes index.
Audience: Ages 7-10
Identifiers: LCCN 2023004069 (print)
LCCN 2023004070 (ebook)
ISBN 9798885245685 (hardcover)
ISBN 9798885245692 (paperback)
ISBN 9798885245708 (ebook)
Subjects: LCSH: White shark—Juvenile literature.
Classification: LCC QL638.95.L3 S37 2024 (print)
LCC QL638.95.L3 (ebook)
DDC 597.3/3—dc23/eng/20230127
LC record available at https://lccn.loc.gov/2023004069
LC ebook record available at https://lccn.loc.gov/2023004070

Editor: Jenna Gleisner
Designer: Molly Ballanger

Photo Credits: Philip Thurston/iStock, cover; Sergey Uryadnikov/Shutterstock, 1; Andrea Izzotti/Shutterstock, 3, 20-21; Ramon Carretero/Shutterstock, 4; Reinhard Dirscherl/age fotostock/SuperStock, 5; Konstantin39/Shutterstock, 6-7; Chase Dekker Wild-Life Images/Getty, 8-9; Willyam Bradberry/Shutterstock, 10-11; Jennifer Mellon Photos/Shutterstock, 12; Blue Planet Archive/Alamy, 13; Minden Pictures/SuperStock, 14-15; David Jenkins/Robert Harding Picture Library/SuperStock, 16-17; wildestanimal/Shutterstock, 18; Dave Fleetham/Pacific Stock - Design Pics/SuperStock, 19; Jayaprasanna T.L/Shutterstock, 23.

Printed in the United States of America at Corporate Graphics in North Mankato, Minnesota.

TABLE OF CONTENTS

CHAPTER 1
Big Fish..4

CHAPTER 2
Powerful Predators.............................12

CHAPTER 3
Amazing Senses..................................18

ACTIVITIES & TOOLS
Try This!..22
Glossary..23
Index...24
To Learn More.....................................24

CHAPTER 1
BIG FISH

A great white shark swims in the ocean. Its powerful tail helps it move through the water.

Great white sharks are dark blue or gray on top. Their undersides are white. This is how they got their name.

CHAPTER 1

Like all sharks, great whites are fish. They use **gills** to breathe. Great whites are the world's biggest **predator** fish. They grow up to 15 feet (4.6 meters) long. They can weigh up to 4,000 pounds (1,800 kilograms)!

TAKE A LOOK!

What are the parts of a great white shark? Take a look!

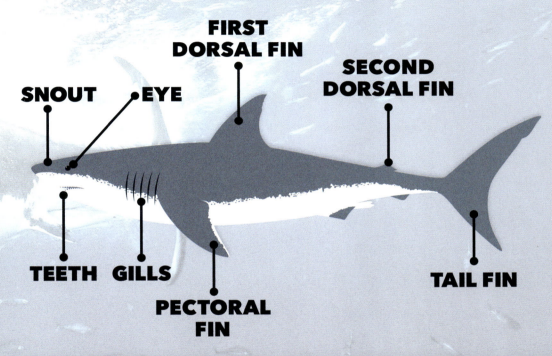

CHAPTER 1   7

Great whites swim in both **shallow** and deep water. Sometimes they swim far out in the ocean. But they usually stay near the **coast**. They find lots of **prey** to eat there.

8 CHAPTER 1

TAKE A LOOK!

Where do great white sharks swim? Take a look!

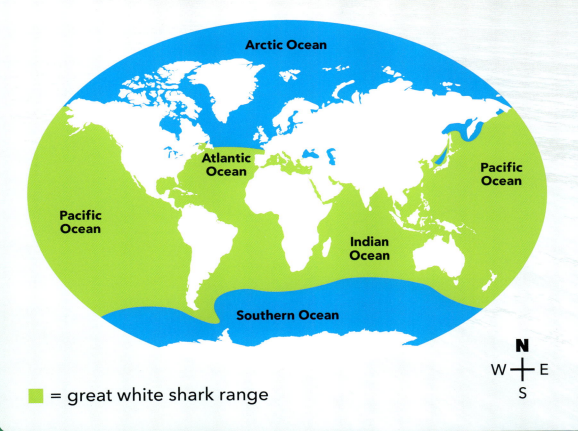

= great white shark range

Every year, great whites **migrate**. When the weather gets cold, they swim south to warmer water. Some migrate 2,500 miles (4,025 kilometers)!

CHAPTER 1

CHAPTER 2
POWERFUL PREDATORS

Adult great whites have very few natural predators. This makes them **apex predators**. They are at the top of the ocean **food chain**.

dead whale

Great whites are **carnivores**. They often hunt seals and sea lions. They also hunt dolphins, squid, sea turtles, and even other sharks! Great whites are also **scavengers**. This means they will eat dead animals, such as whales.

Great whites attack prey from below or behind. They surprise the prey with a big, sudden bite. *Chomp!*

The shark waits for the prey to die. Then rows of large, sharp teeth rip pieces off. The shark swallows the pieces.

DID YOU KNOW?

A great white has up to 300 teeth. The shark loses teeth often. But that's OK! New ones grow in to replace them.

CHAPTER 2

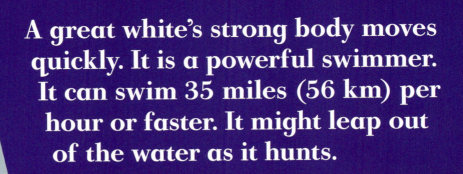

A great white's strong body moves quickly. It is a powerful swimmer. It can swim 35 miles (56 km) per hour or faster. It might leap out of the water as it hunts.

DID YOU KNOW?

Great whites can go one or two months between big meals.

CHAPTER 2

CHAPTER 3
AMAZING SENSES

Strong **senses** help a great white find prey. The shark can see well in the water. It hears well, too. But its strongest sense is smell. A great white can smell one drop of blood floating in 10 billion drops of water! It can smell seals two miles (3.2 km) away.

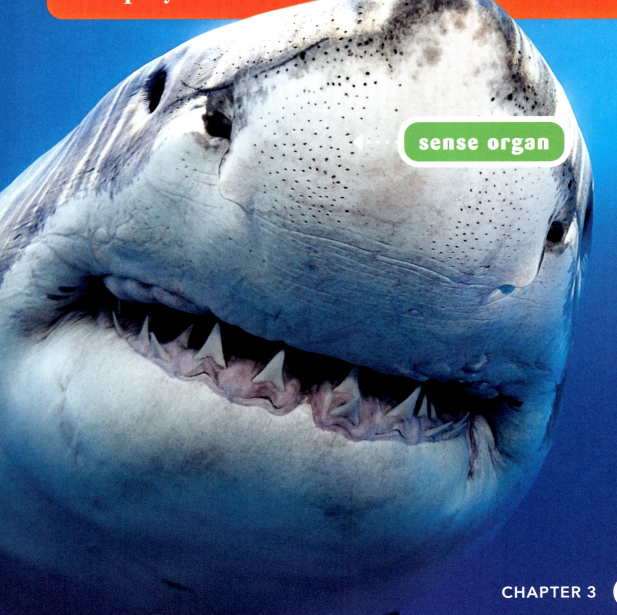

A great white shark has tiny sense **organs** on its snout and jaws. These pick up signals from prey. The signals help the shark find the prey.

sense organ

CHAPTER 3

Great white sharks can swim in water that is too cold for other sharks. How? A great white's body temperature is much warmer than the water. This helps it swim faster and longer as it looks for food.

There is more to discover about great white sharks. What more would you like to learn about them?

DID YOU KNOW?

Baby great white sharks are called pups. An adult female has up to 12 pups at a time. They grow up and can live up to 60 years.

ACTIVITIES & TOOLS

TRY THIS!

OCEAN FOOD CHAIN

Great white shark adults are at the top of the ocean food chain. Learn about food chains in this activity.

What You Need:
- paper
- pen or pencil
- computer or books

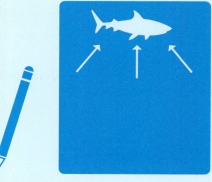

❶ Draw a picture of a great white shark at the top of a piece of paper.

❷ Reread the book to see what kind of animals great white sharks eat.

❸ Draw pictures of the prey below the great white shark.

❹ Draw arrows from the prey that point to the great white shark.

❺ Next, research what kinds of animals the great white shark's prey eat.

❻ Draw those animals near the bottom of your paper. Draw arrows from these animals that point to the animals that eat them.

Look at the food chain you have drawn. Are there more animals at the top or at the bottom? How might changes in the food chain hurt animals in the food chain?

GLOSSARY

apex predators: Predators at the top of a food chain that are not hunted by any other animal.

carnivores: Animals that eat meat.

coast: The land next to an ocean or sea.

food chain: An ordered arrangement of animals and plants in which each feeds on the one below it in the chain.

gills: The pair of organs near a fish's mouth through which it breathes by taking oxygen from water.

migrate: To travel from one place to another place during different times of the year.

organs: Parts of the body that have certain purposes.

predator: An animal that hunts other animals for food.

prey: Animals that are hunted by other animals for food.

scavengers: Animals that eat dead or decaying animals.

senses: The powers living beings use to learn about their surroundings. The five senses are hearing, smell, touch, taste, and sight.

shallow: Not deep.

ACTIVITIES & TOOLS

INDEX

apex predators 12
attack 14
blood 18
body parts 7
body temperature 21
carnivores 13
coast 8
food chain 12
gills 6, 7
hunt 13, 17
leap 17
migrate 10
predator 6, 12
prey 8, 14, 18, 19
pups 21
range 9
scavengers 13
sense organs 19
senses 18
snout 7, 19
tail 4, 7
teeth 7, 14

TO LEARN MORE

Finding more information is as easy as 1, 2, 3.
1. Go to www.factsurfer.com
2. Enter "greatwhitesharks" into the search box.
3. Choose your book to see a list of websites.

24 ACTIVITIES & TOOLS